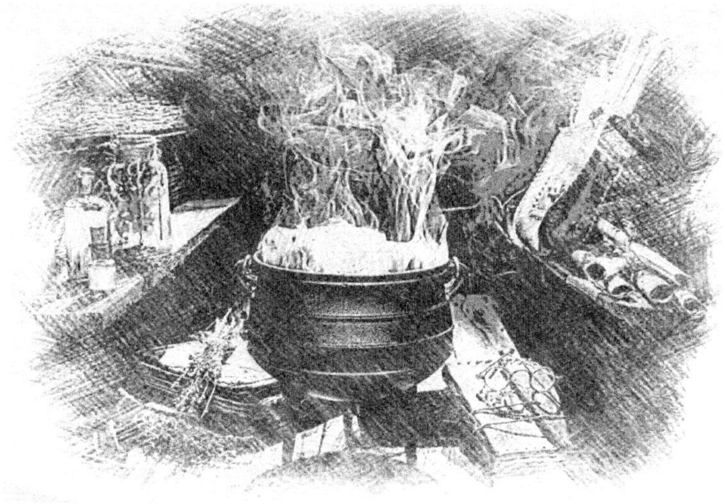

Text Copyright: Beth Murray 2021

Cover Image Copyright: Shutterstock
Cover Design: Beth Murray
Author Photograph: Barry R. Frankish
Internal Photographs Copyright: Shutterstock and Beth Murray
Internal Illustrations Copyright: Beth Murray

## About the Author

Beth Murray lives with her partner, and her daughter in Doncaster, in the north of England. She has been a practicing witch for almost three decades, following both her father and grandfather in its practice.

Witchcraft is a huge part of her life. The title of this book comes from the shop which Beth owns in Doncaster, The Enchanted Way, which sells items relating to Witchcraft, along with more unusual gifts. She also runs basic Witchcraft courses, teaching others how to begin their journeys into the Craft, as well as more specialised development courses.

**Online Shop:**     the-enchanted-way.myshopify.com


**Other titles available from this author:**

Mirror Image
Passions of the Wolf
Midnight Lover
The Unseen Episode and Other Stories

# The Enchanted Way

# The Basics of Witchcraft

By
Beth Murray

Introduction ..................................................................... 6
Part One ........................................................................... 9
The Basic Tools ............................................................... 9
    Basic Tools ................................................................ 10
    The Elements ............................................................. 13
    Cleansing and Grounding ........................................... 16
    Casting a Circle ......................................................... 18
    Crystals ...................................................................... 21
    Plants ......................................................................... 27
    Colours ...................................................................... 30
    Gods and Goddesses .................................................. 32
    The Theban Alphabet ................................................ 44
Part Two ......................................................................... 46
Divination ....................................................................... 46
    Divination .................................................................. 47
    Tarot and Oracle Cards .............................................. 48
    Runes ......................................................................... 55
    Scrying ...................................................................... 66
    Pendulums ................................................................. 67
    Signs & Omens ......................................................... 69
    Fate & Destiny .......................................................... 71
Part Three ....................................................................... 73
Spell-Work ..................................................................... 73
    Candle Magic ............................................................ 75
    Craft Magic ............................................................... 79
    Spell Bracelets/Anklets ............................................. 80
    Sachets ...................................................................... 82
    Spell Boxes ............................................................... 84
    Spell Bottles ............................................................. 85
    Witches' Ladders ...................................................... 86
    Spell Powders ........................................................... 88
Healing Spells ................................................................ 89
    Cleansing House Healing Spell ................................. 90

 Panacea and Apollo Sachet Spell .................................93
 Bracelet Healing Spell ....................................................95
 Candle Healing Spell ......................................................97
 Rune Healing Spell .........................................................99
Protection Spells ....................................................101
 Salt Protection Spell......................................................102
 Animal Protector Spell..................................................105
 Crystal Boundary Spell .................................................107
 Witches' Ladder Protection Spell .................................108
 Deep Freeze Spell .........................................................110
 Queen of Protection Spell .............................................112
 Mirror Protection Spell .................................................113
Success Spells ........................................................114
 Simple Candle Money Spell .........................................115
 Prosperity Powder .........................................................116
 Witches' Bottle and Candle Success Spell ...................117
 Visualisation Success Spell...........................................119
 The World Success Spell ..............................................121
Creating Personal Spells ......................................122
End Note ................................................................127

# Introduction

There are no right or wrong answers when it comes to Witchcraft: it isn't an exact science. Many people who practice the Craft will have heard and read a lot about its use, and, for the most part, it is full of trial and error as they utilise the techniques and words that others have given them, tweaking rituals until it suits them.

Likewise, Witchcraft can be based on a foundation of any religion (or of none!), allowing personal faith to strengthen the words and actions of intent, to send them outwards and cause change. For myself, my experiences of practicing Witchcraft come from a foundation of Paganism, and it is from this perspective that I write this book. Although I haven't always been a Pagan, I have been a practicing pagan for the majority of the years I have spent practicing the Craft.

My lessons and understanding of the Craft have mostly come from books a little like the one you're reading now, yet there is a little family history of which I am blessed to be a part, as my father and (especially) my grandfather both had experience in regards to Witchcraft. However, the family dealings with the Craft weren't revealed to me until I started practicing at around ten/eleven years of age.

My grandfather was a Christian Witch, believing his powers and abilities to come from the Christian God rather than nature, and from the many things that I have heard he had a lot of skill in it. Unfortunately, by the time I came to the Craft, his health had declined to an extent that he no longer practiced. My father is agnostic, and his interest in the subject had faded by the time I began practicing, so my initial instructions on this path came not from blood-family, but from a family of strangers who guided me from the pages of books… and guided me well.

A lot of the things I have learnt from them I have tweaked and tailored to suit my own particular way of practicing, which I will always urge others to do.

I have heard too many witches claim that they work spells "the correct way", and that others are doing them wrong simply because they practice in a different way… I am a firm believer in witchcraft being a personal path, and each person practices it in a unique way, one that works for them. Although you can use the spells included here exactly as they are written, if you prefer to reword them, to dedicate the spells to Goddesses and Gods that are different to the one's I've dedicated them to, to use different ingredients, then please do so – you are the only one who knows what practices are right for you. And if your intuition is guiding you, then go with it!

Many books I have read have "rules" that need to be followed – from what objects to use when marking a sacred circle, to the exact wording of a spell. I disagree with these. So, what is *my* rule for Witchcraft, *my* instruction? Just use whatever feels right to you!

I have written this book as a basic practical introduction to the practices of Witchcraft, a first step along the path, and assume that the reader is new to the subject; if, however, you have experience with Witchcraft, it may serve as a refresher guide, or even add a different view on how you practice.

I hope you find this of some use.

# Part One

# The Basic Tools

Basic Tools
The Elements
Cleansing and Grounding
Casting a Circle
Crystals
Plants
Colours
Gods and Goddesses
The Theban Alphabet

# Basic Tools

I believe that the only thing you really need for Craft work is yourself, and that every item we use are implements that allow us to focus our intent. However, there are some basic tools that are common for witches to use:

Altar – a space that is dedicated specifically to the Craft, and for keeping any ritual items you use. Some people keep only basic items on their altar, others decorate it with the seasonal changes, moving and changing it regularly. How you have your altar is down to what suits you.

Symbols of the Elements – Earth, Air, Fire, Water, and Spirit. A pentagram could be used to represent all of the Elements together, or you could select items for each one individually.

Chalice – for drinking liquids in rituals, and can be used as a symbol of the Goddess, or female aspects.

Athame – a knife used for directing energy, which can also used as a symbol of the God, or male aspects.

Wand – as the Athame, it is used to direct energy

Incense – burn incense to cleanse and rid the area of negative energy build-ups. Incense can also be used to represent the Element of Air.

Candles – a selection can be used as representations of each of the Elements, for the Goddesses and Gods, or for use in specific spells.

Bells – just like incense, bells can be used to rid the area of negative energy and to call positive energies and entities.

Symbols for any Goddesses or Gods you choose to work with or those you feel more connected to.

Crystals – crystals for cleansing, protection, knowledge or anything you're using for Craft work.

Pestle and Mortar – very handy if you are planning on working with herbs, plants and resins.

There are many more things that can be placed on your altar or used for ritual or Spell-work. For example, on my own altar, I have pictures representing what I am currently working towards, and occasionally Tarot Cards and Runes as well.

It's also a good idea to keep a written record of information that you want to keep, your own take on certain things like crystals, herbs and colours, spells that you've used, etc. A lot of people who follow the Craft call a book like this a Book of Shadows. There are some very decorative books out there, with symbols relating to the craft on the covers and page. Simple notebooks are as equally effective.

It common for witches to keep their Book of Shadows private, or solely for members of their Coven, if they are a member of one – this is down to the individual to decide.

# The Elements

There are four physical Elements when working with Witchcraft: Earth, Air, Fire and Water, along with a fifth, non-physical Element of Spirit.

Each of the Elements are associated with directions, colours and attributes, along with the points on the pentagram. There are also Spiritual Beings, known as Elementals, linked with each Element.

Earth is connected to North, to the lower left point of the pentagram, and is associated with green and brown. It is the element of stability, fertility and strength. Working with the Element of Earth is beneficial when beginning or continuing a project, when there is hard work to be completed but rewards to be reaped. Gnomes, the Elementals of Earth and the North, can be called on to request help with work relating to these aspects.

Air is connected to the compass direction of East, and to the top left point of the pentagram, and has yellow and pale orange as its associated colours. It is the element of communication and intelligence, of clarity and acceptance, of information learned. Work with Air for logical and academic knowledge, to help with things like public speaking. Sylphs are the Elementals of the East and Air.

Fire is connected to South, to the lower right point of the pentagram, to reds and fiery orange. It is associated with love, passions and desires, that internal force that drives you forwards to your success. It aids in the motivation to follow the arts. The Elementals of Fire and South are the Salamanders.

Water is the Element of the West, linked to the upper right point on a pentagram, to blue and sea-greens. It is associated with psychic abilities, instinct, and knowledge from internal sources, the learning that come from deep intuition. The Undines are the Elementals of Water and the West and can be called on to aid with these aspects.

Spirit is connected to all directions, the uppermost point of the pentagram, and the colours white, black and purple. There are no Elementals associated with Spirit, but it is linked to the Universe and the Ether.

The Elements can be called on for circle casting, to help guard the corners of the area where magic is worked. They can also be worked with for a specific purpose, as noted above.

Working with the elements for a specific purpose doesn't mean you have to work with just one. Goals are not based on one aspect – things overlap. For example, a spell relating to a successful business venture, Earth could be called on for the determination and steadfastness to work hard, and Fire could be called upon to keep passion for the venture burning, keep motivated, and for its overall success.

# Cleansing and Grounding

<u>Cleansing</u>
Cleansing is a method of readying yourself for ritual work, by eradicating negative energies that may otherwise distract you, leading you to lose focus during your spells.

Depending on what you are preparing to do, cleansing can take place in a couple of ways: either a ritual bath/shower, or by smudging yourself with incense or sage smoke. You can also use visualisations, imagining white or purple light passing over you and removing negativity as it moves.

Regardless of which method you choose, do it with intent, concentrating on ridding yourself of the spiritual and emotional dirt and grime that can build up in day-to-day life, washing away everything that is not useful for the ritual you are planning.

<u>Grounding and Centring</u>
Grounding and centring are two stages of the same thing – grounding helps bring you back to the now, removing any concern of the past or the present; and centring focuses you on the Spell-work you are preparing for.

One way to practice grounding is to simply concentrate on your breathing. Take long, slow and regular breaths, in through the nose and out through the mouth, during which you could visualise the breath in as a shimmering bright white light, and the breath out as a slightly darker colour. Each time your mind begins its chatter, still it by acknowledging the thoughts and then pushing them calmly away. Some people choose to do a longer session of meditation prior to centring, others prefer only a couple of minutes – choose what works for you. This is essentially finding your spiritual balance, a feeling of calmness and stillness. It is that moment of letting go of everything that does not serve you at that moment.

Centring is focussing on the intent of the ritual. Think of what you are aiming to achieve, that final outcome that you are working towards.

# Casting a Circle

Casting a Circle protects you during the casting of spells and during other rituals, as well as helping you to build up the energy and focus it in the right direction.

I still occasionally cast within a corded circle, sometimes with candles, sometimes stones and crystals. I normally use salt if nothing else, but not *always* – it depends what feels right to me *at that moment.* And there are times when I do not cast a circle at all.

Here's a selection of possible items you can use to physically mark a circle:

- cord
- stones/crystals
- salt
- candles
- shells
- feathers
- sand
- leaves/flowers

- ornaments/figurines
- nothing!

Once the Circle has been marked, there is then the ritual of how to cast it, although the act of marking the Circle can be classed as a form of casting it as well. If you want to ritualise the casting of it, however, there are options here too:

Walk around the circle visualising a line of fire or lightning

Walk around the circle and use your athame/wand/hand to direct the energy to the perimeter.

Walk the Circle and chant. Chants can be simple or more structured. There are many books and CDs that are easily available for inspiration for chants, but even chanting a single word or two is effective.

You could ask the guardians of the compass points (North, East, South, West) for protection; any specific Goddess/Gods that you work with; the elements (Earth, Air, Fire, Water); the Elementals.

Generally, chants contain requests of protection for all within the Circle, and requests of added power to the spell/ritual about to be performed. Wording here doesn't have to be precise – and if you stumble over your words (which I do regularly), simply smile and laugh; my belief is that Goddesses and Gods have a sense of humour, and care more about intent than the perfection of how it's articulated.

You may choose not to physically create the Circle, and just create it through visualisation. Sit in what will be the Circle's centre and see/feel it forming around you. You could also visualise it as a complete sphere, a bubble forming over and around you.

# Crystals

There are many different types of crystals. Each has their own energies and properties, promoting positive flows of energy, which can in turn provide physical, emotional and mental healing.

Cleansing crystals before use can help to rid them of any residual energies, especially from others that may have handled them. They don't always need cleansing, so I recommend you cleanse your crystals if you feel you need to.

Like all aspects of the Craft, there is more than one way to cleanse stones and crystals:

Leave the crystals for a short time soaking in salt water**.

Incense sticks/sage smudging: pass the crystals through the smoke – this is my preferred method, as there is no danger of damaging them

Use the elements: sprinkle with salt (Earth) and water (obviously for Water), pass above a flame (Fire) and either pass through incense smoke or breathe onto it (Air).

Cleansing using moving water can be used, washing the stone in a moving stream or the ocean - just remember your own safety when using this method.

Bathing them in either moonlight or sunlight. Simply sit the stones somewhere where the moon or sun will shine on them for a length of time; this can be outside, or on a windowsill, or in the centre of the room if it won't be disturbed. (A lot of people prefer to cleanse their crystals first and then place in moon or sunlight to charge them. As always, listen to your instincts)

**\*\*There are some stones that react badly to salt water, so do a little research on your crystal before using salt water to cleanse them, especially if they are rough cut, not tumbled, as these tend to have cracks and crevices that salt can seep into and damage from the inside. And always rinse them in clean water to remove the salt residue.**

Below are the details of some commonly used crystals and their base meanings.

Hematite – put simply, I *love* these stones! They can be used to help in grounding and for meditations, for protection, and for healing. They help boost energy when you're feeling lethargic or run down.

Clear Quartz – another versatile type of stone. Protection, healing, divination, peacefulness, happiness, success. It is very good for removing negative energies and bringing positive ones.

Citrine – eases nightmares and aids protection, especially in those dark hours. For people who suffer with night-terrors, I've found this can help, and I use it a lot for spells to help resolve sleep problems. Citrine is also a success stone, especially when it concerns business or monetary issues.

Rose Quartz – for love, whether romantic or the love of self, for friendships and families, and to promote calm, and emotional healing, and helps the grieving process.

Tiger's Eye – courage and self-confidence, for luck, especially in financial matters. Very good for anxiety issues, such as social anxiety disorder.

Black Tourmaline – an incredibly powerful stone for protection and driving out negative influences and energies.

Amethyst – much like the rose quartz, use for love as well as for healing and happiness. Also like the rose quartz, it is very good for emotional healing – whereas the rose quartz has a gentler quality to it, the amethyst seems to have more of a punch. It also works as a motivator crystal, giving people energy to accomplish goals and move on from past situations.

Jade – wisdom/knowledge, monetary equilibrium.

Moonstone – boosts psychic ability and intuition, and to connect with the cycles of the moon. It's also very good when working with grief.

Onyx – for protection, and banishment of negative emotions, especially in the home.

Malochite – this is sometimes known as the "midwife stone", and can help ease any discomforts experienced during labour, as well as with menstrual problems. It is also a stone of transformation, of shedding unnecessary and unwanted experiences and habits.

Snowflake Obsidian – this crystal is one of balance. It allows the release of negative attributes, while keeping the lessons they taught. Also a crystal of action and of moving forwards. Can be used for healing, especially with joint pains.

Green Quartz – a great crystal for happiness, creativity and prosperity.

Selenite – a very calming stone which is great for meditation. It's especially good for creating a calming protective space in the home. Also for clarity and clearing confusion.

Blue Banded Agate – reduces stress, builds confidence and overcomes negativity.

Sunstone – a great stone for good luck, fortune and success. Also assists people with Seasonal Affective Disorder (SAD), as it links with the energy of the sun. A very positive crystal.

Labradorite – also known as Merlin's Stone, this is a transformative crystal, providing strength in times of change, and promoting magical growth. With is shimmering colours, Labradorite also stimulates the imagination, and helps alleviate anxiety.

These are the base uses for some commonly used crystals.

I say "base" because each stone has its individual properties. Some hematite stones, for example, may be more tuned in for grounding than for protection; an individual clear quartz may be better suited for healing than for divination.

And if you feel like a stone is better suited for a purpose that is *not* stated anywhere, don't fret too much about it, and go with what you feel is right. Crystals work differently for different people – as each crystal has a unique energy, its own vibration, so does each person; that combination of the two distinctive energies will bring differing results and responses.

Using your intuition to discern what each stone is best used for is key, and the best way to do that is to use the ones you are drawn to.

Once you have chosen your stone, you can charge it with intent. There are a number of ways that stones can be charged for specific purpose:

Bathe in the moonlight on the night of the full moon, or leave in the sunlight through the day – but be aware that some crystals will lose their colour if exposed to sunlight for a long time.

Grasp the stone in your hands and focus on the purpose, intentionally filling it with power for its intended use.

Rub your hands together briskly, as if warming them, until they tingle with energy and heat, all the while focussing on the intent of your spell, then hold the stone between your palms, allowing the energy you generated to pass into it.

# Plants

Plants are very versatile when it comes to Witchcraft: they can be used in Sachets, Witches' Bottles and Spell Boxes. They can be used in creating incenses\*\*, by empowering them and combining them for specific purposes and smouldered on charcoal discs\*\*\* or added to candles. Add them to baths to empower yourself with their properties. Have them growing in and around your home in bring their energies to you. Magical teas\*\* brewed from empowered herbs can be tasty and useful, as can adding them to meals\*\*.

Below is a list of commonly used herbs, plants and resins. It is in no way a complete list, but for those new to the Craft, it's a good one to get started with.

Basil – great for money and prosperity work, as well as for protection and luck.

Rosemary – love and happiness, protection (especially of the home), healing and purification.

Rose – love and friendship, to instil feelings of peacefulness and calm.

Cinnamon – success, power, financial stability, protection, and healing.

Lavender – peaceful sleep, especially for those who suffer with nightmares, reducing feelings of stress, promoting happiness.

Sage – brings wisdom, banishes negativity, promotes healing, promotes spiritual growth.

Dragon's blood – this adds a boost to spells, and is also great for asking for strength and energy, and protection.

Frankincense – the scent of this is beautiful! It is fantastic for protection, spirituality, and purification. This can come in rather large 'drops' which are incredibly difficult to grind – be prepared for a bit of sweating while working with this.

Ginger – attracts money, and good for success, energy and strength.

Peppermint – a brilliant herb for helping with concentration, as well as a healing herb.


Like everything else in Witchcraft, trust your intuitions. If you feel that a herb, plant or resin can be used for a purpose that isn't written in any of the books you've read, then use it for that magical purpose! Don't worry about getting it "wrong" as far as Spell-work goes – but always make sure you adhere to any warnings about consumption**.

When it comes to charging plants and resins, run your fingers through them, lifting them out of the bowl/container and letting them slip out, filling them with the energy of the intent.

** **I do need to stress this, before using any plants, especially ones for consumption, research them thoroughly. Many plants are poisonous if ingested, so before eating, burning or brewing them, check that it's safe to do so. Please be VERY CAREFUL, and look into the properties of each before using them.**

*** **If using charcoal to smoulder incense, use a heat-proof dish designed for very high temperatures and place somewhere safe, as the discs get very hot.**

# Colours

Colours can be a powerful tool for focus when you are doing Spell-work. Below is a basic rundown of colours and their possible uses.

However, your own association with colours are more vital than the list below. If you can't stand blue, for example, using it to aid happiness or calm makes no sense – instead use a colour which actually *does* make you happy or calm; similarly, if you associate monetary growth more with brown (to represent fertile earth), rather than with green (for plants already in growth), then let your own association with specific colours guide you; you will get better results that way.

White – white is a combination of all colours, and so can be used for any purpose and in place of any other colour. It is particularly good for protection and purification.

Black – this is the absence of colour, the balancing force of white. Black can be used for banishing negative feelings or circumstances, and to aid grounding.

Red – red is the colour of energy, strength, and passion, for confidence and success. It's a colour for following your dreams, as well as for passionate love.

Pink – deep love, friendship and compassion, emotional stability and balance.

Yellow – for spells used for intellect and studying, communication, and travel.

Orange – energy and success.

Green – the colour of the abundance of nature, this is excellent for fertility and growth, including development in careers and prosperity.

Blue – healing, both physical and emotional, peace and calming, happiness, creativity and inspiration, psychic development.

Purple – spirituality, psychic power, healing.

Brown – for spells for balance and clear thinking, as well as for spells for animals' wellbeing. Also used for beginning new projects.

# Gods and Goddesses

What follows are a few of the Gods and Goddesses from the dozens of pantheons from around the world, which you may choose to ask assistance from when practicing Witchcraft. It is, by no means, a full list – but will give you a foundation to build on when researching deities to work with.

Some people prefer to work with a single pantheon, however, you may choose to work with whichever deity you feel represents your desired result.

**Ammut – Egyptian.** Ammut is a Goddess of punishment and accountability, with the head of a crocodile, the body of a leopard and the hind quarters of a hippopotamus. She sits in the Hall of Ma'at in the Underworld, where the hearts of the dead are weighed against the Feather of Truth. If the weight is equal to or lighter than the feather, then their hearts are returned to the dead who were then allowed to board Ra's boat and travel to the Field of Reeds. If the heart is too heavy, it is thrown to the floor, where Ammut would devour it, which simultaneously destroyed the soul of the dead.

Call on Ammut for justice, and for consequences for actions.

**Anubis – Egyptian.** Known as the jackal-headed God (although the more recent theory is that he was more likely to be a wolf-headed God since the African golden jackal has been reclassified as the African wolf), Anubis is the Egyptian God of the dead, of lost souls and the helpless.

Call upon Anubis to help assist those who have died, as well as for protection. He can also be asked to send justice and vengeance on those who have wronged us, and send curses back on those who cast them.

**Aphrodite – Greek.** Aphrodite is a Goddess of love, passion, and beauty. After Kronos cut off Uranus's genitals, he cast them into the ocean, where they mixed with the white foam, the aphros; Aphrodite was born of this mixture. The Goddess of Love has the ability to form both true loving attachments and obsessive love.

Call on Aphrodite for promoting self-love, to reignite passion in a relationship, to draw new love (in friendship as well as romantic love), and for recognising your own beauty.

**Apollo – Greek.** Apollo is the God of the Sun, music, prophecy, medicine, and knowledge, and was the son of Zeus and Leto, and twin of Artemis. He is also thought to be a leader to the Muses.

Call on Apollo for healing and health, skills and knowledge, solar and light rituals, and for assistance in divination and prophecy. He can also be asked for help in revealing the truth in all mattes.

**Artemis – Greek.** Artemis is the Goddess of the hunt and of the wilds, and is normally depicted as carrying a bow and arrow, alongside hunting dogs.

Call on Artemis to promote a connection to the wilds, for the protection of animals, and providing sustenance. She is also a Goddess of childbirth (as she helped her mother give birth to her twin, Apollo), and can be asked for assistance for spells for independence and self-reliance, along with aiding focus and intent.

**Asclepius – Greek.** As a God of medicine, healing and doctors, Asclepius is one of the Gods specifically mentioned in the *Hippocratic Oath*, on which doctors used to swear. One part of this oath states "I will keep them from harm and injustice". His staff, known as the Caduceus Wand, has a single snake wrapped around it.

Call on Asclepius for healing, health, and to protect those who provide these things in the mortal world, like doctors and nurses.

**Athena – Greek.** Athena is the Goddess of War, born from Zeus's head fully grown and fully armoured. However, she was known to use diplomacy to avoid fighting where possible. When fighting became the only viable option, she used her extensive skill and strategy to become a formidable opponent. She is also a Goddess of the Arts and Crafts, especially spinning and weaving.

Call on Athena for wisdom and strength, for skill and strategy, law and justice, for the ability to fight when it is necessary, along with the arts and crafts.

**Bast – Egyptian.** Bast is the lioness/cat-headed Goddess of Egypt. She is a protector, defender Goddess, especially fearsome when protecting those who are vulnerable. She is also a Goddess of pregnancy and childbirth.

Call on Bast for protection of animals, the protection of children, and for healthy pregnancies and safe childbirths.

**Brigid – Celtic.** Brigid is a Goddess of Healing, Fertility and Motherhood, as well as a Goddess of Passion and Fire, especially in relation to inspiration for the arts and invention.

Ask for Brigid's assistance for protection, inspiration, and fertility, both in pregnancy and for the fertility of projects to ensure their success. She can also be called on for help with poetry, and healing.

**Cerridwen – Celtic.** Cerridwen is a Goddess of Rebirth and renewal, and as the Keeper of the Cauldron of Knowledge. She is also a Goddess of Wisdom and Magic, especially in regards to herb lore, and is a skilled shape-shifter.

Call on Cerridwen's assistance for wisdom, for aid in any magical workings, and for tapping into your own power to change situations that no longer serve you in order to help you develop something better.

**Cernunnos – Celtic**. God of the Forests and the Wilds. He is a protector of animals and woodlands, and a God of the Hunt, and is also connected to fertility and the passions of physical unions.

Call on Cernunnos for protection, fertility, and to prosper in your projects.

**Circe – Greek.** Circe is a Goddess of Magic and Witchcraft, especially in relation to hedge and kitchen witchcraft. Ask Circe for assistance with magical workings and for practical learning in magical plants.

**Dagda – Celtic.** Dagda is a God of Skill and Wisdom, of the Seasons and Agriculture, and the natural Cycles of life and death.
Call on Dagda for abundance, and for the cycles of fertility, hard work and a prosperous harvest.

**Eir – Norse.** Eir is a Goddess of Healing and Medical Skill.
Call on Eir for health and healing rituals, as well as studies relating to these fields.

**Euthenia – Greek.** Euthenia is a Goddess of abundance and prosperity, both for the home and for businesses.
Call on Euthenia to ensure prosperous and lucrative ventures.

**Freya – Norse.** Freya is the Goddess of Love, Fertility, and Wealth. She is a Goddess of self-assurance, sensuality, and also a Goddess of the Afterlife, as she claims half the souls of those who die in battle and takes them to Fólkvangr.
Call on Freya for spells relating to confidence and strength, prosperity, love and fertility.

**Frigg – Norse.** Frigg is the Goddess of Motherhood, of protective maternal instincts, owing to the lengths she went to in order to try and have her son, Balder, returned from Hel's domain. She is also the Goddess of Matrimony.
Call on Frigg's assistance for child-protection rituals, and for harmony in relationships.

**Gaia – Greek.** Gaia is the original Mother Earth, existing even before the Titans. Although nurturing and comforting, she is also fiercely protective.

Call on Gaia for rituals to heal the earth, seas and forests, as well as for any spell-work for protection, fertility, pregnancy and motherhood, and divine inspiration.

**Hades – Greek.** Hades is the God of the Underworld, with dominion over the souls of the dead. He is also a God of Riches, of possessions.

Call on Hades to help ease the passing of those leaving this life. He can also be asked for help in obtaining financial stability, or to aid in letting go of material possessions/obsessions.

**Hecate – Greek.** Hecate is the Goddess of Witches, associated with magic, witchcraft, and protection. As she guards the crossroads of death, preventing ghosts from causing mischief, she is also connected with discovering the right path when you are at a crossroads in life.

Call on Hecate for issues relating to witchcraft, protection (especially in the cases of women), and when seeking guidance for your path.

*A word of caution about calling on Hecate to administer justice: she does not distinguish between those involved in the situation – she will punish accordingly everyone who holds blame. For example, if you have belittled someone to the point that they lash out, they will be punished for their outburst, but you will also face justice for your own misdemeanours!*

**Hermes – Greek.** Hermes is the messenger of the Gods, who can move swiftly and surely to his destination to deliver information. He can be called on when you need vital information to reach the right person in a timely fashion. He is also articulate, and can be called on to help express yourself in the right manner.

**Hypnos – Greek.** Hypnos is the God of sleep. Through this gentle action, he send rest and respite to people in their times of need, giving them an escape from their woes. He is connected with the night and dark.
Call on him when you need peace and relaxation, for help with insomnia.

**Ilithyia – Greek.** Ilithyia is the Goddess of childbirth, assisting in the healthy birthing of babies, and the skill of midwifes and all who assist in childbirth. She can also be petitioned to help in delaying births for a short time in the event of complications.

**Kali – Hindu.** Kali emphasises the cycle of life, death, and rebirth. Through the complete destruction of the old, she brings about new opportunities and completely new paths. She is also a Goddess of strength, destroying all negative forces and influences.

**Lakshmi – Hindu.** Lakshmi is a Goddess of wealth, fortune and prosperity. She is also a Goddess of love, beauty, and joy. Through these things, she brings fulfilment and contentment in all areas, combining everything to create something close to perfection.

**Loki – Norse.** Loki is a God of Mischief, of Chaos. Loki is intelligent, but rarely looks at the long-term repercussions of his actions.
Call on Loki when you need to add drastic change into your life. Although Loki may bring this change is likely to be completely unexpected, and sometimes devastating, ways,

**Ma'at – Egyptian.** Ma'at is the Goddess of Truth, Balance, and Justice. After death, the souls of the dead travel to Ma'at's Hall, where their hearts are removed and weighed against the Feather of Truth.
Call on Ma'at for justice, truth, and for moving on from past mistakes.

**Mimir – Norse.** Mimir is a God of Prophecy, Knowledge and Wisdom.
Call on Mimir when vital truths and guidance are needed, and also for gaining knowledge and learning.

**The Moirai – Greek.** The Fates, as they are also known, decide the life-spans of all mortals and the Gods. Clotho spins the thread of life for each being, Lachesis measures it and decides the length of life, and Atropos cuts the thread, ultimately deciding when and how each dies.
You can call on The Moirai for help in realising your true potential. Atropos can be called upon to help those who are close to passing from this life do so with ease and without suffering.

**Morpheus – Greek.** The God of Dreams, Morpheus created the dreams that were sent to mortals, passing along prophetic signs and divine knowledge. This makes him a deity to ask for assistance in receiving and understanding prophetic dreams.

**The Morrigan – Celtic.** The Morrigan is a Battle Goddess, powerful, strong and skilled, as well as a talented shape-shifter.
Ask the Morrigan for assistance with strength in times of struggle, or when battles need to be fought, for

wisdom in knowing the best way to gain the advantage. Also call on The Morrigan to shape-shift from what you are into what you want to become.

**The Muses – Greek.** There are nine Muses, who are Goddesses of the Arts, and while each of the nine have their own speciality, calling on the Muses collectively will aid in inspiration and determination to persevere in your arts.

**Nemesis – Greek.** Nemesis is the Goddess of justice and retribution. She punishes those who knowingly, or through self-centred tendencies, causes harm to others.

She can be called on to bring justice, as well as for strength in difficult situations.

**Nereus – Greek. Nereus** is a God of the Waters, who can shapeshift and is gifted in foretelling future events, but only to those who will heed his words and take action based on them.

Call on Nereus to connect with the oceans, rivers and lakes, and to discover actionable truths of the future.

**Nyx – Greek.** Nyx resides in the depths of the Underworld, and is the Goddess of the Night. She is both beautiful and strong, and holds dominion over all animals – both natural and supernatural – that belong to the night.

Call on Nyx for strength, power, and to connect with the night. As a fierce defender, especially for children, she can also be asked for assistance in protection spell-work.

**Oya – African.** Oya is the Goddess of the Weather, especially those of possible destructive potential, such as lightning, fire, tornados. She is also a Goddess of Women, and transformation, a warrior.

Call on Oya to connect with your strong feminine power and potential, for protection (especially of women), and to help enhance your leadership qualities. She will also aid you in clearing away everything that no longer serves you, leaving a path for new growth.

**Poseidon – Greek.** Poseidon is the God and Ruler of the Oceans, Storms, and Earthquakes.

He can be called on to ensure safe travel over the waters. He can also be of assistance for navigating stormy situations, and when you are feeling lost and without direction. As the "Earth-Shaker", he can be petitioned for help when you need to make drastic changes.

**Ra – Egyptian.** Ra is the God of the Sun, and represents the nurturing quality of the sun.

Ra is associated with spell-work relating to the success of projects, fertility and growth.

**Rhea – Greek.** Rhea is a Goddess of Fertility, especially female fertility, and of Motherhood.

She can be asked for assistance in all matters of having, raising and caring for children.

**Rhiannon – Celtic.** Rhiannon is the Horse Goddess, associated with the Moon, and with Sorcery. She is strong- and fair-minded, intelligent and strategic, beautiful and generous.

Rhiannon can be asked to help in the protection of horses, as well as the protection of people, especially those who are down-trodden. She can encourage the discarding of feelings of victimisation, and for strength in doing the right thing.

**Sekhmet – Egyptian.** Sekhmet is the lion-headed Goddess. She is a fierce protector, a Goddess of war, and is strong and determined, allowing none to take advantage of her or of those she defends.
Call on Sekhmet when you need to find courage to do the right thing, or in times when you need to defend others. She is also someone to call on for independence and resilience.

**Selene – Greek.** The Titan Goddess of the Moon, who drives the Moon across the sky in a chariot pulled by white horses.
As a Goddess of menstruation, fertility, pregnancy and childbirth, she can be called for assistance in all of these matters, with connecting to the moon and the night, and the constant changing cycles of life, death and rebirth.

**Skadi – Norse.** Skadi is the Winter Goddess, a skilled huntress who prefers the winter mountains to any other location. She is strong, knowledgeable, and independent.
She can be called upon for endurance during harsh times and times of scarcity, and for connecting to the winter times.

**Thoth – Egyptian God.** Thoth, the ibis-headed God, is the scribe of the Gods, prizing truth above all. In the Hall of Ma'at, it was he who took record of the weighing of the heart after a person's death, and was the one who ultimately decided whether the heart weighed more or less than the Feather of Truth.

He can be called on in matters of truth, justice, and knowledge, and also for help with literature and the written word.

**Tyr – Norse God.** Tyr is connected with war and justice, of strength and overcoming difficulties. He is connected with honouring promises and faithfulness.

Call on Tyr to ensure that people keep their word, as well as for finding solutions in difficult situations.

**Vesta – Roman.** Vesta is the Goddess of hearth and home, bringing warmth, comfort and harmony.

Associated with a candle always burning, honour her with candle/fire magic to make changes in the home and to bring domestic bliss and contentment.

**Yemaya – African Goddess.** Yemaya is an orisha Goddess of the ocean. Thought to have been the creator of all life in the waters, she is an ultimate mother deity, nurturing but just.

At any time that you feel you are constantly fighting against the tide, ask Yemaya to take you to your shore – this may happen on a gentle tide, or a tidal-wave. She can also be asked for help in matters of protection and motherhood.

# The Theban Alphabet

The Theban Alphabet is an alphabet designed to hide magical writings, for example within a Book of Shadows, and for use in written spells.

There seems to be some dispute about when the Theban Alphabet was first used, and there are a few variations on some of the actual symbols utlilsed. On the following page is one of the versions of the symbols used.

An example of translation of a spell (from Part 3), using the symbols shown:

To all negativity sent my way,
this mirror shall reflect back to the sender.

| | | | | | |
|---|---|---|---|---|---|
| A | ᛏ | B | ᚴ | C | ᛘ |
| D | ᛗ | E | ᛉ | F | ᛠ |
| G | ᚢ | H | ᛣ | I | ᚢ |
| J | ᚢ | K | ᛖ | L | ᛉ |
| M | ᚴ | N | ᛚ | O | ᛄ |
| P | ᚸ | Q | ᛩ | R | ᛗ |
| S | ᚷ | T | ᛉ | U | ᛦ |
| V | ᛦ | W | ᛦᛦ | X | ᚢᛘ |
| Y | ᛘ | Z | ᛘ | (End of sentence) | ⌘ |

# Part Two
# Divination

Divination
Signs and Omens
Fate and Destiny

# Divination

The subject of divination always brings to my mind a stereotypical image: a woman in a shawl, sitting on a stool within a dark and incense-filled room, gazing raptly at a crystal ball with a Tarot reading spread out before her. I have used Tarot cards since I was a child – the use of the cards was actually my induction into the craft – and very rarely does that image match how I work with divination!

Divination is a way of looking into the past, present and future with the use of tools. What I will add here, is that the items we use for divination is the same as with Spell-work – the real power comes from us, the items we use are ways of focussing our intent and thoughts; and in the case of divination, these tools help us to cut through the background noise and focus on specific information and insight.

There are many different methods, some of which I'll be discussing in this chapter, and it comes down to what you are drawn to. My personal preference is with the Tarot and Oracle cards; I have used other methods, but I always come back to those – so it's with those that I will begin with.

# Tarot and Oracle Cards

Tarot Cards
There are hundreds, if not thousands, of different designs of Tarot, ranging from light fantasy, dark gothic, animals, and even films. Choosing a deck that will work for you is a matter of instinct, and you will respond better to those you are drawn to.

There is a theory regarding purchase of Tarot Cards, that you should never buy your own, that they should always be gifted to you. Although this may be accurate for a few people, more than half of the twenty-three decks I own, I have bought for myself, and I work better with those than the ones gifted to me. As with all aspects of Witchcraft, if you're drawn to something, there's a reason. The majority of people I know who also work with Tarot Cards, have had the same experience.

The Tarot Deck is split into two groups: The Minor Arcana and the Major Arcana.

The Minor Arcana resembles a pack of playing cards, containing four suits – Cups, Pentacles, Wands, Swords – and numbered one through ten, plus four court cards – Paige, Knight, Queen and King.

The Major Arcana are what the majority of people think of when they think of the Tarot: Twenty-two cards, containing ones such as The Wheel of Fortune, The Lovers, Death, The World.

Learning to work with the Tarot can be daunting, with seventy-eight cards to learn the meanings for, especially with so many books specialising in Tarot that seem to have contradictory messages. However, there are some ways to make it a little easier:

The four suits address certain aspects:

Cups, represent emotions and relationships, friendship and love.
Pentacles represent finances and material wealth, prosperity and financial successes.
Wands represent creativity, work, hobbies, studies, the things that we do that require action.
Swords represent the intellectual, the logical, conflict and resolutions.

Each grouping of cards (the Major Arcana and the four individual suits) tells a story: a new beginning, building towards minor success, encountering a setback, then a regrouping, re-evaluation, and ultimately a completion.

Let's use the Wands as an example: The Ace of Wands, represents a brand new creative path, stepping forth with desire, passions, a clean slate with nothing to hold you back.

The Two of Wands shows that passion merging with focus, planning on how to best reach your goals, which continues building with the Three of Wands, and the Four of Wands is that moment of success – not complete success, but that first little victory that means you're getting somewhere.

Five of Wands is a moment of set-back, of things going contrary to your plans, followed by the Six of Wands where you are able to get back on your feet with new lessons learned that you can use to go forwards.

Success keeps building through the cards until you reach the Ten of Wands, final completion, complete success.

Each of the suits have the same flow – fresh starts filled with passion, merging with skill and purpose, a first victory, followed by an obstacle, then the continuation after applying your new knowledge, to arrive at a moment of achievement.

The court cards follow this rhythm too, only relating to people in your life (perhaps yourself):

The Paige is a person full of innocence and passion, full of inspiration.

The Knight is someone who combines the passion of The Paige with a high level of skill.

The Queen represents someone who has passion, skill, and the focus to put both into action.

The King combines all the passion, skill, desire with wisdom and objectivity to know when each needs to be used.

The Major Arcana also follows this pattern – Card 0, The Fool, youthful exuberance at the start of the path, moving through patterns of success and loss, most notably The Lightning Struck Tower, a new beginning marked by the Death card, then building to Card 21, The World – that ultimate success of the cycle completed.

Once you've learned the basics of the cards, here's where the tricky bit comes in – to rely on your intuition when doing a reading, and not be hung up on the written definitions of each card, to essentially learn the cards and then forget their meanings: once you get used to doing readings, you will discover that the meanings change with each reading. Always trust your intuition with a reading – the power, after all, comes from you and not the cards.

Oracle Cards
Oracle Cards work in the same way as Tarot, but are not limited by the standard Tarot set-up: there can be any number of cards in a deck, and they are based on practically anything. There are decks that are based on animals, some with gods and goddesses, energies, past life influences, angelic influences, the moon cycles, and many others. As with the Tarot, the sets that will work best for you are the ones you feel drawn to.

Because of the elaborate differences between the decks, it is difficult to give a run down on all of them here – but most sets come with an instruction booklet with the basic meanings, and I would give the same advice as with the Tarot Cards – learn the basics, then let your intuition take the lead.

Reading the Cards
When I do readings I generally use both Tarot and Oracle Decks – the Tarot for answering questions posed to it, and the Oracle for advice on the best way to proceed, but this is just my preference for working with them.

There are so many different ways to lay out Tarot cards during a reading, some simple and some more complex. Here a few examples:

Three Card Spread
This first is a very simple three card spread.
Concentrate on the question you want answered and shuffle the Tarot cards.
Lay 3 cards down from the top of the deck, I tend to work right to left. Some books recommend you read them as 1 = past, 2 = present, 3 = future. However I find it more informative to read them all as one, simply answering the question without any temporal order; your intuition will let you know if it's past, present, future.
It is a simple spread, but I've found it very effective.

## Crossroads Spread

This spread is ideal when you are feeling lost about what direction you should take, at a metaphorical crossroads where you can turn left, right or go straight ahead, with no idea which would be best.

Card 1 – Place directly in front of you. This represents you, as you are right now.

Card 2 – Place slightly above Card 1 and to the left – this is the first path you could take.

Card 3 – Place on the right, opposite Card 2 – this is the second path open to you.

Card 4 – Place above Card 1 – this is the path you are on now and could continue to follow.

## Nine Card Spread

This spread addresses how the past situations are contributing to your future paths, and is laid out in three rows of three cards.

Row One – the past experiences that are have contributed to where you are now.

Row Two – the present influences that are currently important.

Row Three – the future based on the past and present.

Try different spreads and see what works best for you, the same with the different Tarot decks – you'll find the one for you.

Regardless of the layouts you use, when cards are dropped while being shuffled, read those as part of the reading, as an additional bit of information that is needed.

# Runes

Rune stones come in all shapes and sizes, and can be inscribed on wood, pebbles, crystals, and there are also sets done in card form, for those who work better with Tarot or Oracle cards. They can be used for divination, a connection to our own unconscious, and also used in Spell-work.

ᛗ Mannaz – The Self

Live in the present by clearing away anything negative from the past that doesn't serve you. Complete tasks for the joy of the task, rather than any benefit you will receive for it. Break bad habits, and be the best version of yourself that you can be.

ᚷ Gebo – Gift

A partnership of two equals, both as important as the other. Work together, but do not let yourself be eclipsed or taken advantage of. Gebo is the gift of freedom.

ᚠ Ansuz – Signals

Receiving information in a way that will be advantageous, seeing information as it is rather than how we wish it to be. This allows us to find our true path, allowing a new life to unfold.

ᛟ Othila – Inheritance

This rune represents all you have been born into, your inheritance and birthright. This may be physical, cultural, intellectual. Some of these things need to be embraced, held close to you. There are other parts of your inherited past that you should separate from, anything negative that no longer serves who you are becoming. This could be in negative views held by your family, bad habits you've picked up from them, or actual physical objects that you no longer need.

ᚢ Uruz – Courage

This is a time of change. You've outgrown your old life, and it's now time to create something new, which takes courage and strength. Right now is the time of rest, of letting the old life die away, ready to build something new. Also a rune for health and healing.

## Perth – Initiation

A rune of initiation, of opening up to gain knowledge and wisdom. This is internal knowledge, information not shared, profound secrets that cause an awakening in the spirit.

## Nauthiz - Constraint

Things are difficult, and you need to exercise restraint. This could mean a drastic change in income, resulting in the need to be wiser with your finances. Or it could be difficulties in relationships where you are needed to be more patient and supportive. There are holdups on the way, and now is the time to persevere in the knowledge that eventually it will get better.

## Inguz - Fertility

A time of completions and readying for new beginnings – a birth, a new career, a brand new path. You are preparing to make that new start, the moment is almost here, and you have the strength and the skill to stride out on your path with confidence.

### Eihwaz – Defence

This is a time to assess the situation you are in, and to make plans to overcome the difficulties you now face. Once you know exactly what the blockages are in moving forwards, what defences you have to build to secure what you have, you can make your plans – that way, you will be ready to put them into practice when the time is right. Patience here is key.

### Algiz – Protection

This rune is emotional protection as well as physical. You do this by admitting your feelings, embracing them so they can be processed, strengthening yourself, which in turn makes you more capable of securing more protection. The symbol is the sign of an elk with three horns, horns which can defend as well as attack in order to protect.

### Fehu – Possessions

Fehu is a symbol of prosperity, financial stability, and luck. Ambitions are realised, success achieved. Don't squander what you receive, though; remember to count your blessings, but allow your good fortune to help others. As you've achieved success, help others achieve their own.

ᚹ  Wunjo - Joy

Joy and blessings in the material, emotional and relationships Things are great – perhaps not perfect, but you are at a time of a sense of completion and contentment. Spiritual well-being and a sense of purpose.

ᛃ  Jera – Harvest

Success is on its way, but it requires time and hard work. You are at the point of spring and planting the seeds, and a season of growth is needed before your harvest is ready to be gathered, but as long as you water those seeds and tend to the plants, the harvest will be fruitful.

ᚲ  Kano - Torch

Kano is the light that shines in the darkness, lighting your way and revealing all to you. You will gain clarity, enlightenment and knowledge. It shows and opens doors that you can step through, away from old patterns and towards new ones.

### ↑ Teiwaz – Warrior

Teiwas is a spear, which slices through the air, cutting through chaos and uncertainty. This weapon of the warrior will guide you through conflicts, through every battle you need to face, granting you the strength to see all things through as you walk towards you goal with trust and purpose.

### ᛒ Berkana – Growth

Berkana has the shape of a woman in the late stages of pregnancy – full breasts and full belly. This is a rune of progression, growth, a blossoming that cannot be rushed, but it almost imminent. Use this time to prepare for the eventual birth, to tidy and get things in order, to nurture what you are growing and to make sure that things are set up ready.

## Ehwaz – Movement

The horse pulling the sun across the sky, you are moving yourself onwards to something incredible. This is a positive transition, one of empowered action, and you can run with abandonment, knowing that the pit-falls have been overcome.

## Laguz – Flow

Don't fight against the flow of the tide, you are only going to exhaust yourself. It is time to follow the cycles that ebb and flow, listen to your intuition – you will know when to move forwards and when to rest. Also a rune of merging, of the conscious and unconscious, logic and intuition, a marriage of self and all your aspects. Harmony of self and of others, balance and merging of relationships.

## Hagalaz - Hail

Disruption of plans, a storm that comes from nowhere to knock your plans on their head. Relationships falter or fail, business plans go awry, things you thought were stable can disappear. It initialises an awakening, of the self or the situation, and forces you to break away from what you thought you were supposed to be or be doing. Although you cannot control the storm, you are empowered by how you deal with it – you can seek shelter, you can batten down the hatches and wait for it to pass, continue to work through despite the storm, or walk through the storm to find something else. Your responses are your own, you have that choice, and after the storm ends, you will see how much you have grown.

## Raido - Communication

Remember there are always two sides to the story. Communication is necessary to come to an understanding, and a resolution. All aspects must be taken into consideration before you decide where to go from here. Once that understanding has been reached, of looking at all aspects, either start or continue your personal journey. This is also a rune of journeys, travel and endurance, knowing that you have everything you need.

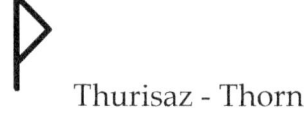

## Thurisaz - Thorn

Thurisaz is a chaotic rune, that is sharp and painful like the thorn on a rose. It is also a powerful gateway rune that can allow you to step through, transforming you into something completely different.

## Dagaz – Breakthrough

You've done it, you've reached that moment of first victory – it may not be a completion of your project, but you can now see that that completion is close to hand. Your potential now is limitless that you've made this transformation. You are urged to not give up, but to keep up the momentum you have built.

## Isa – Ice

This is a rune of standing still, of non-movement. Projects may freeze as if they are trapped in ice, and will not begin to move on until the thaw. Surrender to the forced inaction, and don't be tempted to push ahead. Be patient and wait until things begin to move onwards in their own time.

## Sowelu – Sun

Strength and light, warming and nurturing. A Rune of wholeness, and triumph, of reaching a destination after a long journey.

The Unknowable – Destiny
This is a blank rune, with no markings. It is full of potential, of unanswered questions. There is no actions for you to decide on, no information to be understood, at least not yet. This is a stone of waiting for more information to come available. You cannot control what has yet to be formed, and you cannot take action until the options present themselves.

You can use the same method as Tarot Cards in order to read the runes – focus on your question, then pull the stones and lay them out in the same spreads.

You can also use a cloth or board, with markings for different areas of life – relationships, work, finances, personal growth – and gather all the runes in your hands and cast them onto the layout. Discard any that fall outside the marked area of the cloth, and also those that fall face-down. Read the Runes that remain, taking note of in which aspect they have fallen into.

On the following page is a basic layout design for Rune Casting.

| Personal Growth | Career |
|---|---|
| Finances | Relationships |

# Scrying

The art of Scrying is divination using reflective surfaces, for example in still water, crystal balls or mirrors. I know many people who use clear crystal balls for Scrying, however I don't have much luck with them. My own preference is for a black mirror or a large piece of dark crystal.

As scrying can take a while, its best to sit in a comfortable position.

Have a single candle lighting the room, preferably placed behind the surface you are using to prevent any glare reflecting whilst still giving you enough light to be effective.

It can take awhile to get the hang of Scrying, as you have to gaze at the surface while simultaneously relaxing your eyes so that you're not actually focussing on it, but rather seeing *through* it. It is very similar to inducing a state of self-hypnosis, which allows you to view what's shown.

# Pendulums

Pendulums are weighted items suspended on a chain or cord. Many pendulums are crystals or cones of metal. However, you can also use personal items as pendulums, such as a ring threaded onto a chain, or a pendant. The only important aspect of it is that it is weighted enough to hang.

When used for divination purposes, many people use a "yes/no" system in order to gain information.
   Pendulums move in different ways for different people, so it's always best to ask the first time you use your chosen item to show you the movement for "yes" and the movement for "no".

You can also design or buy a cloth or board. Designs vary, from very basic yes/no/rephrase, to more in depth laid out with letters and numbers.
   Hold the pendulum over the centre of the layout and ask you question, noting what the movement indicates.

On the following page is a simple board design.

# Pendulum Chart

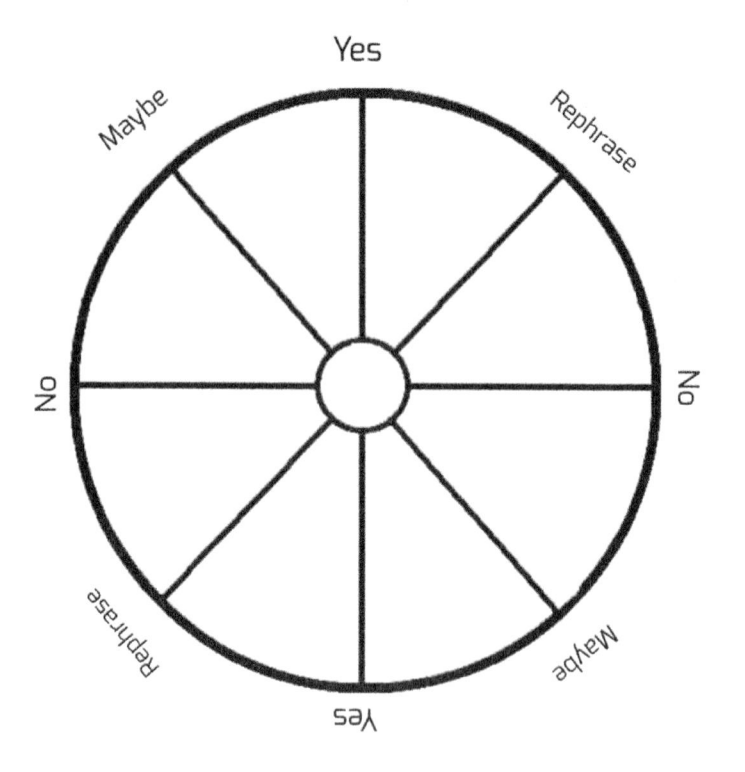

- Yes
- Rephrase
- No
- Maybe
- Yes
- Rephrase
- No
- Maybe

# Signs & Omens

There are many books with lists of signs and omens and their meanings, just as there are many books on dream interpretation. In both cases, I don't always agree with the interpretations that are presented.

I think that both portents and dream interpretations are subjective: Regardless of what causes these omens (the universe, Gods or Goddesses, angels or spirits), I believe that the signs are sent in a way that you can understand and interpret them; that they are based on your own perceptions and understandings - they are completely personal.

In many books, for example, snakes are seen as omens of betrayal and danger, possibly based on the Bible's assertion that a snake tempted Eve in Eden. Yet for me, snakes are symbols of the mystical and of deep knowledge, as well as portents for change and adaptability. For some, dragons are seen as symbols of greed and destruction, while for me they represent magic and protection.

Trust your own feelings on what the appearance of signs and omens say to you, and don't worry about it being different to how others would interpret them.

As to what it is that makes the presence of something a sign or omen: there is a feeling that accompanies the appearance of a sign or omen, a sensation of deep meaning and of something on its way, that differentiates it from it being just an object that you've seen.

Like many things in Witchcraft, allow your own experiences to guide you in your interpretation and practice.

# Fate & Destiny

There seems to be a dichotomy in regards to the perception of fate and destiny, falling into two distinct camps: the first believe that everything is predetermined, from the largest action to the smallest, and the second that believe that everything is a result of free-will and nothing is set.

What you come to believe is down to your own perception, understandings and beliefs.

Personally, I think there's a mixture of the two. I see the events in life that there is always a choice as to the path you take, but there are some events that will occur regardless of which route you move along.

Almost as though there are direct routes and scenic routes – which one you choose is down to you, and sometimes it takes you in a completely new direction, and sometimes you end up in the exact same destination as you would have if you'd taken the other route.

I've added this here, at the end of the divination section of the book, because I think it's important to remember that, no matter what your divination shows about the future, it will only show the future of the path that you are currently on – you can always turn on to another course and change your future experiences.

# Part Three
# Spell-Work

Candle Magic
Craft Magic
Healing Spells
Protection Spells
Success Spells
Creating Personal Spells

One of the main things to remember about working spells is that you can perform them in any way that suits you – the spells that you learn can be tweaked to your own preference. Spells are a way of praying, of asking for assistance – for some, it's praying to the ancient deities, or to the universe, or even to ourselves as we manifest with our own energy.

If a spell is dedicated to a specific God or Goddess but you feel connected to another for the purpose, then simply change the name of the deity you are asking for help. Or if you don't work with pantheons, you can send it out to the Universe or to the Earth.

The same goes for specific wordings of the spells themselves. There are rituals written in rhyme, while others are basic sentences details what action is needed: spells don't have to follow any specific format. They can be simple or elaborate, involve pages or rhyming wording, or be totally silent.

It all depends on what works best for you.

Don't agonise yourself over the "perfect" wording of a spell, either, or of the consequences of making the incorrect gesture at the wrong time. It is your intent that works the spell, and as long as you know what it is that you want to achieve, and focus on that outcome, your intent will carry it along.

I relate Spell-work to shooting an arrow. You take aim (focus on your intent), pull the string back (work the spell), and let the arrow fly (send the spell outwards). Then trust that it will hit its mark.

# Candle Magic

First thing. It doesn't matter what type of candle you use. If all you have in the house is a birthday-cake candle, then charge it, light it and use it! After all, if you've ever made a wish on the candle of a birthday cake, that's a form of candle magic.

The only differences in candle types are the burn times. If the spell you are working requires it to be burned for an hour or so every day for, say, a week, than a dinner candle would probably be best; for a spell which lasts for about an hour for only a single session, then spell candles would be perfect for it. Jar candles, tapers, tea-lights, shop-bought or homemade – it's entirely up to you.

## Making Candles

Making a candle from scratch can be beautifully fulfilling, and you can dedicate them to a particular purpose from the moment of creation.

For this you need:
- Moulds – metal or thick plastic, and available in a huge assortment of shapes and sizes, or

simple tealight moulds in which the candles can be burned.

- A double boiler – a pan of boiling/hot water which holds another bowl containing the wax to be melted. This stops the wax getting wet and also prevents it burning.

- Heat-proof gloves – so that you can pick up the inner bowl to pour your wax into the moulds.

- A method of holding the wick steady in the centre of the mould as the wax sets around it. You can buy slips of plastic that sit on top of the moulds, with a hole in the centre for the wick to pass through. Alternatively, a small strip of cardboard with a hole in the middle for the wick to pass through to do the same job, although try to make sure it doesn't completely cover the top of the mould, as this can sometimes increase the cooling times.

- Wax beads – these can be paraffin-based, beeswax, or soya wax.

- Wicks and wick-bases – the circular metal bases that the wicks are threaded through prevents the wick moving off-centre while setting and makes it safer to burn.

- Essential oils – a great way of imbuing the candles with purpose. Fragrance oils also work well.

- Herbs – a great way to add intent to the candle at the point of creation.

- Colouring – natural colorants, wax colourings, or even crayon shavings.

How to Make Candles:

Melt the wax in the double boiler, and stir in any of the additional elements for intent that you choose to use, consciously recognising what energies you are adding to it.

Put the wicks in the moulds, carefully fill with wax and allow it to set. For best results, leave somewhere cool overnight. Then remove from the moulds, or leave in if creating tealight candles.

## How to Use Candles:

Inscribe symbols or words into the candles, engraving your request or need into it. Then charge your candles in the same way as with the stones and crystals, transferring energy and intent from yourself to the candle. Hold the candles and concentrate, imagining the energy passing into the candle; or build the energy in your hands by rubbing the palms together and then transferring it to the candle.

Anoint the candle with oil, simply coating the candle thinly. Vegetable oil is fantastic, but you can also use base oil or essential oils that correspond with the intent. (Have a towel or a few sheets of kitchen roll handy for this, because your hands will get greasy.)

Roll the candle in herbs that correspond with the intent until it's coated.

Then work your spell.

# Craft Magic

With Craft Magic, you work with your hands, taking separate elements and putting them together until something new and unique has come into being. For me, Craft Magic sums up all aspects of magic – all energies combining to create something new, to create a change.

I love working with Craft Magic, because it is so versatile – there are hundreds, thousands, of types of creative methods that can be utilised for magical use; basically, anything that can be created can be used as a centre-point for Witchcraft.

# Spell Bracelets/Anklets

A huge plus about this technique is that they can be worn unassumingly, and unless you explain the purpose behind it, it merely looks like a home-crafted bracelet! Therefore, if you work a spell on behalf of someone else, they can wear the bracelet without enduring any form of derision.

For this you need:
Nine embroidery threads in the colours that correspond to your desired outcome. For example:
A spell bracelet designed for attainting substantial work as an artist, you may choose to use three strands each of green (for prosperity), blue (for creativity and inspiration) and red (for passion and success).
A spell for physical healing could contain five strands of blue (for healing), two strands of white (for purification) and two strands of black (to banish negative attributes that can contribute to an illness).

Directions:

Measure each thread by wrapping them loosely around your wrist or ankle four and a half times. Knot them together at one end.

Arrange the threads into three groups each containing three strands, in whatever combination of colour you prefer. From left to right, we'll call these groups A, B and C.

Now you need to braid the groups together. Cross the right section over to the middle, changing the order to ACB, then cross the left section over to the middle, reordering them to CAB.

Repeat this, holding the strands taunt, until the whole length is braided, then securely knot the ends together.

While braiding, concentrate on the reason for the spell, speaking any words or chants that you've decided upon.

The bracelet can be worn when the spell needs to be active – for example, if using a bracelet to gain employment, wear it when actively looking for work, filling out application forms and attending interviews etcetera; or it can be worn consistently until the threads come apart naturally, which is ideal for healing spells.

# Sachets

The first thing I need to say about using sachets is this: they do not need to be embroidered masterpieces of breath-taking skill in order to work. I am not a seamstress, the only stitches I can complete are basic and normally not beautifully rendered. Any runes or symbols I add to them are roughly executed. It doesn't matter if you can embroider artwork that would rival Arachne, or if nobody but yourself is able to identify what it's supposed to be. It's the *act of creating* it that matters along with the intent you add to it.

For this method for Craft Magic, you need a long rectangle of cloth, whatever size you deem appropriate for where you intend to keep the finished product – sachets to be kept in the house are normally larger than those made to be carried in a pocket or bag. Use a colour corresponding to the intent.

Embroider or write symbols or words which indicate its use, for example, Inguz for fertility, Algiz for protection, pentagram for protection or magical power, caduceus for healing.

Once you've decorated as you want, fold it in half and sew closed two of the open edges, leaving one side open. Add all of the components you wish to include, before sewing it completely closed. This could include herbs, stones, and items personal to who the spell is for, such as a photograph or lock of hair.

While making the sachet, say any spell that you've written or any words that you feel are right for your intent.

Set the finished sachet wherever you feel is most appropriate: in the case of fertility, place it under the bed or pillow of those trying to conceive; for protection of a home, place it near the main door, or near the centre of the house.

# Spell Boxes

You can use any kind of box for Spell Boxes. If you are burying you box in the earth, biodegradable boxes are perfect to allow the earth to absorb the spell. These are especially good for success spells, with the intent that as the box disintegrates, the spell is released.

If you intend to keep the box for a long time, small wooden or denser card boxes can be used and adapted.

If you are skilled in woodwork, you can also build your box from scratch, adding details for intent during the process of creating it.

Engrave or paint symbols on the box, inside, outside, or both.

Add inside everything that you wish to include as you would with sachets, and then seal the box. This can be done with candle wax (a candle that has been charged for the same purpose can give an extra boost), or use ribbon or thread to tie it securely closed.

# Spell Bottles

Also known as "Witches' Bottles", they follow the same technique as Sachets and Spell Boxes. Decorate the glass with symbols and words, and fill with plants, stones and anything else you wish to use.

Spells Bottles usually also contain a small scroll of paper, written on which is your desired outcome.

While placing items into the bottle, speak your spell, close the bottle with a cork or lid, and seal it with wax. If you are doing a candle spell alongside a Spell Bottle, use the wax from that candle to seal the bottle.

# Witches' Ladders

The first part of this technique follows the same directions as the Spell Bracelets, with the addition of nine feathers, tied along its length.

You will need:
- nine embroidery threads in the colours that correspond to your desired outcome, each about 30-40cm in length.
- nine feathers – these can be natural or coloured to add extra colour correspondence.

Directions:

Arrange the threads into three groups each containing three strands, in whatever combination of colour you prefer. From left to right, we'll call these groups A, B and C.

Now you need to braid the groups together. Cross the right section over to the middle, changing the order to ACB, then cross the left section over to the middle, reordering them to CAB.

Repeat this, holding the strands taunt, until the whole length is braided, then securely knot the ends together. While braiding, concentrate on the reason for the spell, speaking any words or chants that you've decided upon.

Once you've braided the entire length, securely knot the ends together.

Knot the feathers along the length, keeping your focus on what you are adding to the spell.

When all the feathers have been added, hang the Witches' Ladder where it is needed.

# Spell Powders

Spell Powders are a mixture of herbs, plants and resins, ground as fine as possible, and is very similar to incense. Unlike incense, however, these mixtures aren't smouldered but sprinkled.

Adding coloured sand or biodegradable glitter adds a little sparkle to it, and also adds colour association to the spell to give it an extra boost.

Add Spell Powders to Spell Boxes, Bottles or Sachets as part of larger rituals.

Protection Spell Powders can be created for use when casting a Circle for larger rituals.

Sprinkling Prosperity Spell Powders at the threshold of the door you use the most to enter and you're your home will bring money to you.

Sprinkling a Success Spell Powder in the place where you work or in your till to bring you success for your business.

# Healing Spells

With all magical workings, you need to keep in mind that there are many factors in play, of which you are only one.

Your spells may make an illness go into remission, or it may work by nudging a doctor to read the right article at the right time, which could inspire them to find the correct diagnosis and treatment.

Witchcraft can work obviously and/or subtly. Once a spell is performed, you have *no control* as to how it manifests, and you need to have faith that it will work in the best way.

# Cleansing House Healing Spell

This spell needs to be performed over several days or nights, requiring an hour or so each time.

For this you need:
- a photograph of the subject of the spell, looking healthy and happy.

Ritual:

Take a few moments gazing at the photograph, while you centre and focus on the illness that you are trying to rid them of.

Cast your circle and sit as comfortably as you can, while ensuring that you're not likely to fall asleep. Then close your eyes.

Picture the person the ritual is for, try and see them as clearly as you can. Now picture a house to represent them. See every aspect of it – how many floors it has, how many windows, what material it is built from, what colour the front door is. Does it appear (from the outside, at least) to be a cottage, a mansion, or a 2-up-2-down? The house is a representation of the person, and each room is a part of their physical being.

Once you have the house in focus, picture a large hazardous-waste container beside it, open and empty, bright yellow, with hazard symbols on it.

Walk into the house, and begin to look for signs of the illness within the house, which will be seen as rubble or mounds of dirt, or a mass that needs removing. Take your time and search the house carefully, looking in each room. You will probably find that there are more rooms inside the house than looks possible from the outside, yet try not to rush this. As the illness may be based in more than one room, continue looking even after you've found it, noting all rooms it lies in. Doing this will probably take the majority of the first session.

After finding the illness-debris, you need to remove it. This is the part that takes the time. Removing the debris is done by hand, and must be carried out of the house and put in the hazardous-waste container. There are no shortcuts for this, no wheelbarrows or shovels to help lighten the load.

It takes time plus a lot of strength and energy. When you begin to feel drained or start to lose concentration, then you must stop, no matter how much you have done or how much there is still to do. Close the door to the room(s) containing the illness to prevent it spreading. Mark a pentagram, a rune of healing, or a caduceus on each, as well as on the front door to the house, to prevent it from spreading.

Close and secure the waste-container, marking it with a symbol to contain the illness you've removed so far.

Open your eyes and open your circle. Afterwards, have a snack and a drink of water (or cup of tea!) to bring your energy levels up a little.

Repeat this once a day/night, depending on your preference, until the rubble has been completely removed.

# Panacea and Apollo Sachet Spell

For this you need:
- A photograph of the person for whom you're working the spell, one that shows them looking healthy and happy
- A rectangle of blue cloth, natural fibres if possible
- Purple thread, plus needle for sewing
- Hematite stone
- A copy of the spell written in blue ink
- Bay leaves, sandalwood, cinnamon, thyme, sage, dragon's blood.

Ritual:

Sew or draw a caduceus (a staff with a snake entwined around it) or a rune of healing onto the cloth, and create the sachet, while chanting:

"Health returns, quickly heal".

Add the photograph, stone and plants then sew closed the sachet.

Hold the finished sachet and speak the spell:
"Weaved and crafted, health return;
Upon you illness now has no hold!
The flame of health strongly burns
And returns to you three-fold!
By Panacea and Apollo, by Moon and Sun;
As I will, so shall it be done!"

Give the sachet to the person for whom it was made, with instructions for it to be placed somewhere they will see it every day.

# Bracelet Healing Spell

For this you need:
- Three blue threads
- Three purple threads
- Three white threads

Ritual:
Hold them together and say:

> "Blue to heal illness,
> Purple to maintain health,
> White to purify, within and without."

Tie the ends together and separate into three groups, either into groups of colour or into groups containing one of each colour.

Braid them together, saying:

> "Braided now together,
> From nine into one;
> The Power weaved forever,
> Now it shall be done.
> From all within and all without,
> As below and so above,

Balance within and all about,
In trust, faith and love.
I weave this magic into one.
By my will shall it be done!"

Once finished, hold the bracelet, focussing on the person it is meant for, and say:

"Braided now together,
Together now they're bound;
Power weaved forever,
Health and well-being now found.
By Goddess and God,
By Moon and Sun,
By Dark and Light,
Shall it be done!
By Earth, by Sky, by Flame, by Sea,
So be it done, so mote it be!"

It should be worn constantly. Once the bracelet falls off, the spell is complete, and the remnants of it can be discarded, or used within a box/sachet/pouch spell for continued health.

# Candle Healing Spell

For this you need:
- A photograph of the person you're doing the spell for
- A blue candle
- A pin to inscribe it
- Lighter or matches
- Anointing oil, plus towel
- Thyme, sage and cinnamon

Ritual:

Charge the candle and herbs for healing. Using the pin, inscribe the candle with the name of the person you're working the spell for along with a caduceus, and with a pentagram.

Anoint it with oil and roll it in the herbs until it is coated. Place it securely on your altar, if you have one, or in a special place where it can burn safely. Place the photograph to the side or underneath it.

Light the candle, and say:

> "As the flame flickers
> And the candle burns,

> Health is sent to you
> As the Wheel turns.
> Its healing light
> To you goes,
> Wellbeing and strength
> To you flows.
> So mote it be!"

Let the candle burn down.

If you wanted to use this candle spell as part of a larger healing ritual, you can use the candle stub (once it has cooled) as an ingredient in a healing sachet or healing box.

# Rune Healing Spell

For this you need:
- A blue candle
- A needle to inscribe the candle
- Lighter or matches
- A piece of paper
- A blue pen
- A safe place to burn the paper (for example, a fireplace, chiminea, or fire pit)

Ritual:

Inscribe the rune Uruz onto the candle, and on the opposite side, the name of the person the spell is for.

Using the pen, write the rune Uruz on one side of the paper and the person's name on the reverse.

Light the candle, and use the flame to light the piece of paper. Place the burning paper where it can burn safely, and say:

"As this fire consumes,
so all illness and disease also be consumed."

Place the candle somewhere it can burn safely.

# Protection Spells

This section deals with protection spells. This can be self-protection, or safe-guarding of your family, your home or your business.

Regardless of any spells you do for protection, remember to keep your common sense in regards to safety.

# Salt Protection Spell

A basic spell for protecting all that lies within the boundaries of your home (or business).

For this you need:
- A large amount of salt, either rock salt, sea salt or table salt – alternatively, use crushed egg shells.

Ritual:

First, choose a place at which to begin this ritual. You could choose the northern-most point of the boundary, or at a gate, or the most hidden point of the boundary. It is entirely up to you, and is only important to consciously decide this so that you know exactly where you need to go in order to close the circle.

Stand at your start point and ask the Goddess, God and Spirit to turn away all who would do harm all areas within the boundary:

"Goddess of the moon and night, may none who wish harm enter within this boundary. So mote it be.

"God of the sun and the day, may none who wish harm enter within this boundary. So mote it be.
"Spirit of all that was or could ever be, may none who wish harm enter within this boundary. So mote it be."

Trace the boundaries of the property with salt/egg shell, ensuring that the 'circle' ends at the point you started (if your home is semi-detached or terraced, and you physically cannot take the circle around your entire home, continue the circle of salt/egg shell inside, along the adjoining wall, moving through all of the downstairs rooms that are connected to the other house).

Trace the boundaries twice more, this time with your athame or wand (if you don't use an athame or wand, clasp your hands together and extend both index fingers), pointing at the boundary rather than sprinkling salt. Visualise a protective barrier forming between the inside of your boundary and outside.

At the completion of all three circles, and back at your starting point, raise your athame or hands above your head and say:

"As above!"

Rest the tip of dagger or your fingers to the ground and say:

"So below!"

You can also visualise physical barriers being created, such as a strong wall, a barrier of thorns, or a circle of fire.

For added protection of the house specifically, sprinkle salt/egg shell at the threshold of each door that leads into your home, and trace pentagrams on the inside of all of the windows and exterior doors.

# Animal Protector Spell

For this spell you need to choose a creature that, for you, represents protection, ferocity and strength. Any creature will do – lion, crocodile, dragon, griffin, whatever feels right to you.

Ritual:

Try and see your chosen creature in as many details as you can, but don't be too concerned if it's nothing more than a shape or shadow – as long as you know it's there and can see or feel it, then that's enough.

Walk it along your boundaries, moving slowly and steadily, letting it learn its new territory. If you live in a semi-detached or terraced house, see it moving through the walls to the inside of the house and walk it through your home before returning outside again, and continue walking until you come back to the starting place.

Tell it that this is now its territory, and ask it to protect its new terrain, to defend against any who wishes harm on you or yours, or those that would take what isn't theirs to take. Be respectful and ask, don't command. Thank the animal and allow it to fade, knowing that it is still there and will help guard your home.

# Crystal Boundary Spell

For this you need:
- Five black tourmaline crystals, of any size.

Ritual:
Cleanse all five crystals, and charge them with the intent of protection.

Place one at each compass point along the boundary of your property, burying them beneath the ground or placing it in a plant pot at the site, whichever is preferred or better suited to the layout of your garden.

If a compass point is inside your home, place the crystal in a plant pot on that spot, or on the floor tucked to one side so it won't get disturbed or knocked out of place.

The fifth crystal, place in the centre of your home.

# Witches' Ladder Protection Spell

For this you need:
- Five white threads
- Four black threads
- Four white feathers
- Five black feathers

Ritual:
Hold all the threads together and say,

"White to protect, black to banish all negativity".

As you braid together, say:

"Braided now together,
From nine into one;
Protection weaved forever,
Now it shall be done.
From all within and all without,
As below and so above,
Balanced within and all about
In trust, faith and love.
I weave this magic into one.

> By my will it shall be done!"

After braiding, tie your nine feathers along its length.

As you attach each feather, say:

> "With this string and with this feather,
> Protection to my home I tether."

Once finished, hold it, concentrating on the purpose for the spell, and say:

> "Braided now together,
> Together now they're bound.
> Power weaved forever
> Protection lays all around.
> By Nyx and by Hestia,
> By Moon and Sun,
> By Dark and Light,
> Shall it be done!
> By Earth, by Sky, by Flame, by Sea,
> So be it done, so mote it be!"

Hang it high in the place you feel protection is needed.

# Deep Freeze Spell

This spell is suited for protection against a specific person to stop them from causing any negative influence in your life.

For this you need:
- A photograph of the person causing you problems (this needs to be the person on their own, not in a group)
- Wide black ribbon
- A freezer bag or container
- A black pen

Ritual:
Take a moment to think of the negative way they are impacting on your life, every problem they are causing, and think of the effects that this is having on your own happiness and well-being.

On the back of the photo, draw the rune Isa and write:

"You are bound from causing harm"

Bind the photo with the black ribbon so that it is completely covered, while saying:

"With Soteria's protection, your harmful ways will end.
Under her watchful eyes, no pain from you can reach me.
As Soteria's protective heart reaches over me and mine,
Negativity from you is blocked, over land and over sea."

Place the bound photograph inside the freezer bag and put it in the back of your freezer, and forget about it.

If you don't have a photograph of the person, write their name on one side of a piece of paper and the rune and spell on the reverse.

# Queen of Protection Spell

For this you will need:
- The Queen of Swords from a Tarot Deck

Ritual:
Focus on the card picture, at the Queen of Swords. Focus on the power of the woman wielding the sword, on the strength, ferocity and protection this image brings.

Say:
"Goddess Morrigan, she of the three faces,
Warrior Woman who wields the Sword.
Protect and guard this place, and all who dwell within.
By your strength and ferocity may you protect all here from harm."

Place the Queen of Swords in the centre of the home or over the inside threshold of the main door.

# Mirror Protection Spell

For this you will need:
- A mirror of any size
- A way of attaching it to a wall or banister (glue, hook etcetera)
- Glass pen, paint marker pen, or permanent marker pen

Ritual:

Mark a pentagram or Rune Teiwaz over the front surface of the glass.

On the wall or doorframe opposite the main door to your home, so that it directly reflects the entrance, attach the mirror.

Once it is secured, say:

> "To all negativity sent my way,
> this mirror shall reflect back to the sender."

# Success Spells

Practicing visualisations for personal success is important, in everyday life as well as magical, but you have to remember to put the work in too.

Spells aside, it ultimately comes down to you. If you do a spell to get a career you dream of but don't look for the chance, how can the forces you've invoked lead you to the perfect opportunity? If you do a spell for success but make no attempts to chase it, then there will be no way for the end goal to come about.
    Work your spells, but remember to also take action.

# Simple Candle Money Spell

For this you need:
- A green candle, and pin to inscribe it
- Vegetable oil, and towel
- Dried basil
- Lighter or matches

Ritual:

Inscribe the candle with your name and the exact amount of money you need, no more. If you have an unexpected or urgent bill for £157, then that is what you mark it with – not £150, or £160, use the exact amount; focus on your need being met perfectly.

Anoint the candle with the oil and then roll it in the basil.

Fix it into the holder and light it. Look into the flame and say the following three times:

> "Money in my hand will grow,
> To my side, money will flow."

Allow the candle to burn down safely.

# Prosperity Powder

For this you need:
- A mortar and pestle
- Dried Basil
- Dried Cinnamon bark
- Dragon's Blood Resin

Ritual:

Grind together dried basil, dried cinnamon, and a small amount of dragon's blood, until it is as fine as you can make it. As you blend them together, focus on being able to pay bills as soon as you receive them, of clearing any debt, and of being able to indulge in some luxuries.

Sprinkle at the threshold of the door to your home that you use most regularly, or to business entrances. Add grains to purses, wallets or tills to ensure money flows into them.

# Witches' Bottle and Candle Success Spell

For this you need:
- An orange or red candle
- Lighter or matches
- Vegetable oil, and towel
- Prosperity Powder
- A small glass bottle
- dried cinnamon, rosemary, basil
- clear quartz, sunstone, citrine
- Paints or paper and pens
- Any charms or personal items that represent your goal - for example, if you're a dancer, maybe an image or small charm of a ballet shoe; if a writer, maybe an image or small charm of a typewriter or pen
- Orange or red ribbon or thread
- Paper and pen

Ritual:
Anoint the candle with your prosperity powder, and set it burning.

Fill the glass bottle with the dried herbs, and add the crystal.

Draw an image of a brilliantly shining sun on the paper and place it inside the bottle. Also add the items that represent your goal –.

Say:
>"With these objects, of nature's gifts,
>I attract success to me;
>To fulfil the goals of my desire,
>Harming none, so mote it be!"

Seal with wax from the candle and use orange and red ribbon/thread to decorate. Allow the candle to burn down.

Set the bottle somewhere you will see it every day, to give you added motivation to continue working towards your goal.

# Visualisation Success Spell

With this spell, it is vital that you see *your own perception* of what your success would mean to you, and not the way that others would imagine it for you. Ignore the hopes of others for this - this type of visualisation spell is totally subjective, is yours and yours alone. Would it make you wealthy? Would it give you a personal sense of achievement and satisfaction? Would success for you mean travelling abroad or building foundations anywhere specific?

For this you need:
- A quiet and comfortable place to sit.

Ritual:

Sit within a circle and focus on your goal, specifically attaining the success you long for - if you wish to succeed in the arts, for example as a painter, see your paintings hanging pride of place in a gallery; for success in sports, picture yourself winning races and standing on a podium. For success in business, see yourself making the kind of deals that you could only make at a high point in your career, sitting in a large office.

Take your time, and visualise it as though it has already come to be.

# The World Success Spell

For this you will need:
- The World card from a Tarot Deck (or a duplicate of one if you'd prefer)
- Cinnamon essential oil

Ritual:
Hold The World card and focus on what success you are hoping to achieve, every positive thing that success will bring you.

Add two drops of cinnamon oil to the card, one on each side.

Continue holding the card, continue visualising the positive way success will alter your life, and say:

"Goddess Fortuna, who brings success to ventures,
May you to bless my deeds with success and triumph,
May you guide my actions so that I achieve my goals and reap good fortune.
Grant me your blessings, so mote it be."

Place the card in a place associated with your goals.

# Creating Personal Spells

This section is dedicated to an aspect of Witchcraft that the majority of practitioners, especially those new the Craft, are most worried about: creating spells from scratch. What you need to remember is this: *someone* at some point designed that spell that you have used with confidence and surety of success – and there is no guarantee that they were any more adept at spell casting than you are.

*You* are the source of your power, the techniques are merely ways of focussing your intent in the most effective way, and the herbs, colours, stones all work as cues to your unconscious, a nudge to ensure that your intent is pointing the right way.

There is no 'minimum-time-spent' when deciding on how long a ritual should take: they can be as long or short as you wish them to be, as simple or as elaborate as you want to make them. If you have a gift for memorizing spells, then you may decide to write something lengthy and wordy; if your memory (like mine) makes Dory from *Finding Nemo* look like a memory champion, then simplify it – nothing will break your focus more than worrying over remembering fifty-plus lines of prose.

## Step One – Identifying Need

> The starting point for ritual writing is the reason, the intent, behind it. Why do you feel that a magical helping-hand is important? Try and be specific in your reasoning, precise in what you are wanting.

## Step Two – Who Can Help

> Is there a specific deity that could aid in your spell? Regardless of the pantheons you look at, all deities have their characteristic attributes, things that they are known for. Artemis is the Greek Goddess of the wilds and the hunt. She was usually evoked to ensure a successful hunt, a hunt that would provide meat to feed a family or community. She was also believed to punish those who hunted for reasons other than necessity, who took her precious gifts and wasted them. Another example from the Greek pantheon is Hecate, whose 'speciality' is justice. However, her justice truly is blind, and *all* who have done wrong in that situation will be held accountable, even if that includes the one who asked for her help. An Egyptian God, Thoth, is partly known for giving the gift of writing, and could be called upon for times where help is needed in putting

words eloquently down on paper – which, as a writer, is something I can appreciate!

You could ask for help from the compass directions, the elements or the Elementals for their assistance, either collectively or just the ones more in tune with your spell.

Or maybe you don't want to ask any individual entity for help, but want to just send it outwards.

**Step Three – Which Technique Do You Want To Use**
Which technique appeals to you for the spell you're considering? Do you see yourself making a bracelet for this purpose, or is it burning a candle that draws your attention? Maybe you want to combine different techniques, perhaps make a witches' bottle whilst in a circle of powder that you've created. Perhaps you will need to look at the appropriateness of some of the techniques – maybe you have an inquisitive pet that could knock a lit candle over, making candle work unsafe.

Allow your instincts to guide you as to what will work better for you for that spell. And remember that, even if this spell works well, the next time you wish to cast a spell for a similar reason you may feel drawn to a different technique for it – these are not, and will never be, set in stone.

**Step Four – What Words Will You Use**
If you are doing a spell and wish to include words and chants, you first need to choose how you want to organise your request. There are a few ways to do this:

Say what is missing or what needs changing, and then say in which way you want it to transform. In money spells for example, you could say what lack of money means to you (inability to pay bills etc), and then state what you need to be able to fulfil those needs.

Speak words as if your request has already been fulfilled. For a health spell, you could say nothing of the illness or its negative impact on your life, but speak only of being healthy and well, as if it has already happened.

Simply chanting a word or groups of words that represents your need (example, 'success is mine, success is mine, success is mine') can also be effective, and can become a mantra for you.

There is no one technique better than the other, and you will find yourself using different styles at different times. Don't worry about it being right or wrong; if you listen to your intuition, then it will be the right style.

And that's the extent of ritual writing! Seriously, there's nothing more to it than that. Four steps and you've created a personal spell.

# End Note

Firstly, I want to thank you for allowing me to journey with you, even for such a short time. I can only hope that I have been a guide of some use and have added something positive to your individual path.

Secondly, I urge you to read as many books as you can on the subjects contained here, and listen to as many views as you can - but always keep in mind that the beauty of Witchcraft is that there aren't any hard and fast rules or regulations. Use your intuition, trust your instincts, let your morals and your conscience guide you on how you move forwards, and use what you feel is right for you.

Thirdly, always enjoy the Craft, however you choose to practice it!

And lastly, in order to see anything in life you have to be open to the chance. On the following page is a photo that I took a few years ago, while walking along a pavement that I've walked a few hundred times before. I asked for some reassurances during a difficult time, a sign that I was on the right path. All I did was briefly glance to my left, and I received my answer.

Beauty, magic and wonder is there if you open your eyes and allow yourself to see it.

Image © Beth Murray 2014

**Blessings on you and the paths you tread.
Beth Murray 20/03/2021**

I hope you have enjoyed this book, and found it to be of some use on your magical journey.

If you're able, please leave a review for it on Amazon, and let me know what you think – I'm always grateful for feedback.

To those interested in my other published works, follow me on Facebook to keep up to date with publications.

facebook.com/BethMurrayAuthor

Printed in Great Britain
by Amazon